What did God promise to give Abraham and Sa[...]
to find out. Thank God for keeping all His promises.

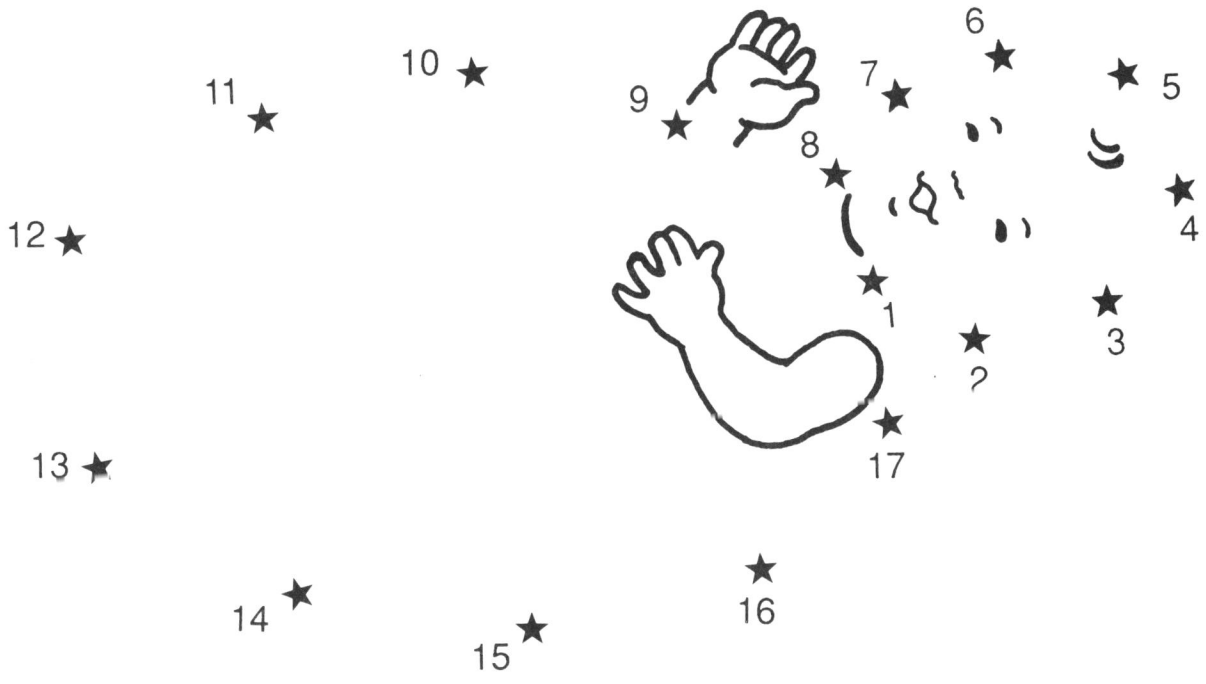

10

11

9

6

7

5

8

12

4

1

3

?

17

13

16

14

15

1

God gave Isaac and Rebekah twin boys named Esau and Jacob.
Though they were twins, they liked different things. How many
different things can you find in the pictures of the two boys?
Color the picture and give Esau and Jacob different clothes to wear.
Thank God for making you special.

Esau

Jacob

2

Jacob had twelve sons. Circle the picture with the right number of boys.
How many children are in your family? Draw a picture of your family
in the empty box.

3

Jacob gave his son Joseph a special coat with long sleeves. Decorate a beautiful coat for Joseph. Which favorite clothes do you like to wear?

4

Baby Moses' mother hid him in a basket in the river. Draw tall grass to hide him as he floats in the water. Color the rest of the picture.

Big sister Miriam watched her little brother Moses to be sure that he was safe. Color the picture to see where she is hiding.

w = blue   x = green
y = yellow   z = brown

God gave His children bread called *manna* to eat as they traveled to their new home in the Promised Land. What good food does God give you? Draw it on the plate.

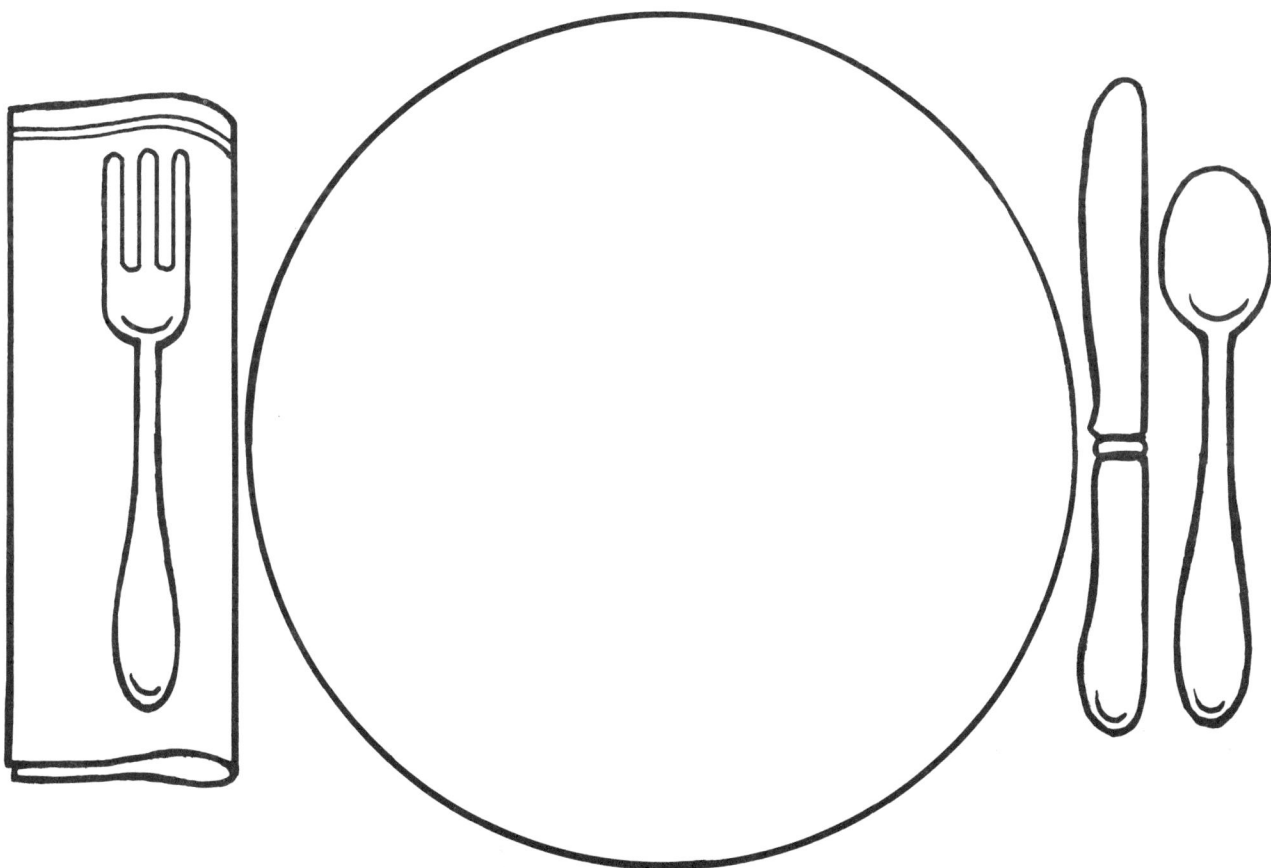

7

God answered Hannah's prayer and gave her a son named Samuel. When Samuel was old enough, Hannah took him to the church. Draw a line showing them the way to go. What do you like to do at church?

8

CPH © 1993

Samuel's mother visited Samuel at the church every year and brought him a special present. Connect the dots to see what it was.

2
4
1
5
3
12
6
11
10
7
9
8

9

CPH © 1993

Grandmother Naomi must have been very happy when baby Obed was born to Ruth and Boaz. Draw a picture of you with your grandparents. Then give them the picture.

Obed and Naomi

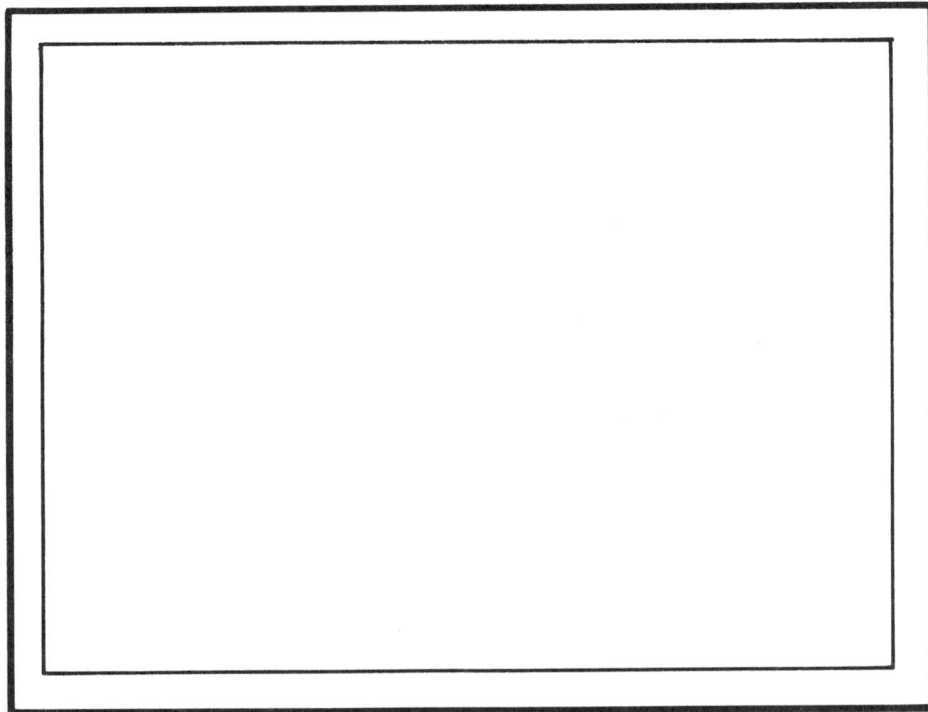

My Grandparents and Me

10

David took good care of his father's sheep. Help David lead his sheep to a new field of grass. Thank God for taking good care of you.

11

David and Jonathan were good friends. Trace the lines to see whose arrow landed closer to the big rock. Who are your good friends? What can you tell them about Jesus?

David

Jonathan

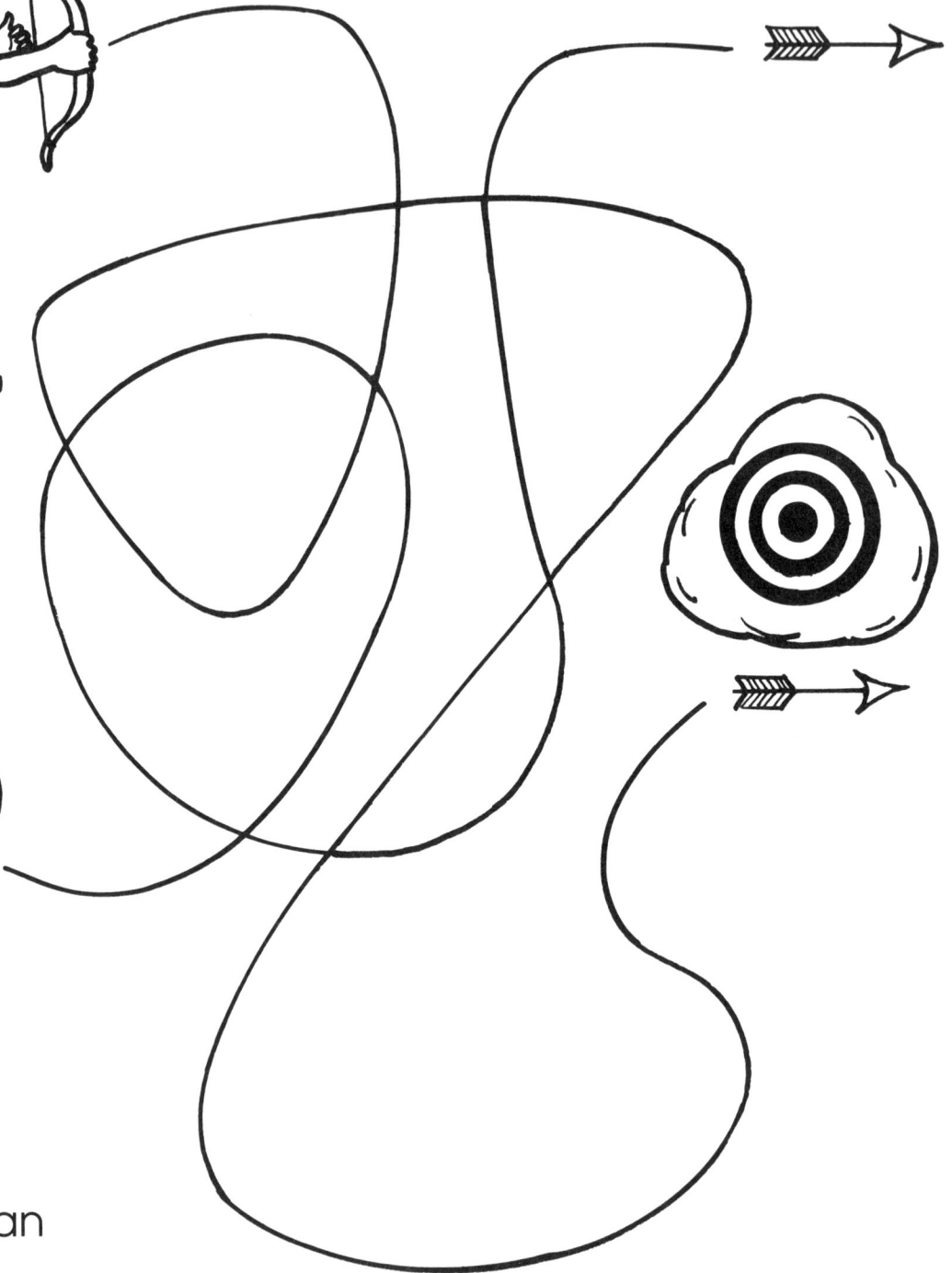

12

A young servant girl worked as a slave for a man named Naaman. When he became very sick, she told Naaman's wife that the prophet Elisha, who lived in her country, would cure him. What did Elisha tell Naaman to do?

13

When Joash was little, his aunt hid him in the temple to keep him safe.
Connect the dots to see Joash's temple home.

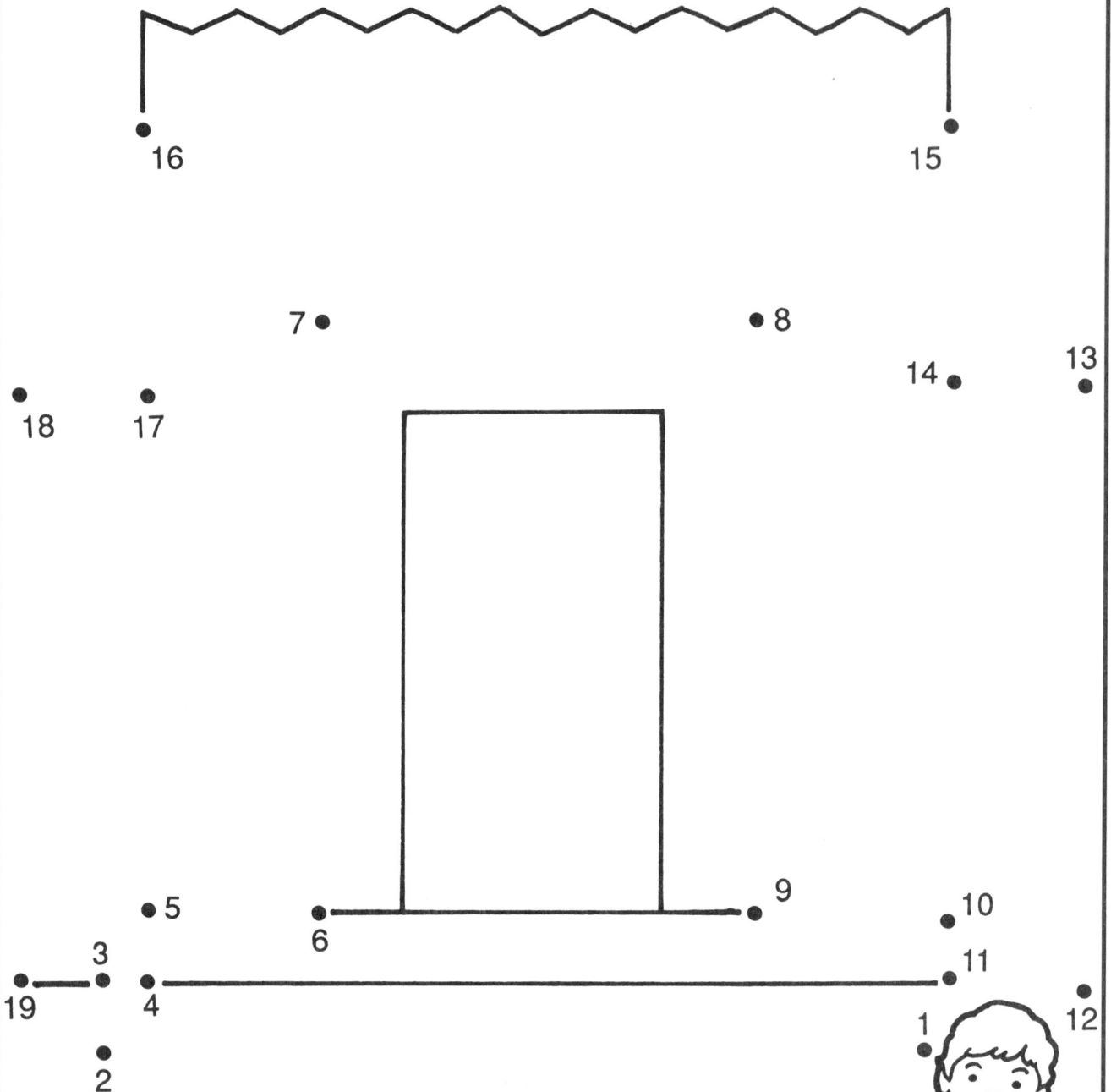

16

15

7

8

14

13

18

17

5

9

10

6

11

3

19

4

1

12

2

Joash became king of Judah when he was seven years old.
Connect the dots to see his crown. Decorate it with bright jewels.

6

4

8

2

5

7

10

3

9

13

12

1

14

11

15

Daniel and three other young men were taken to a land far from their home. They would eat only food that God wanted them to eat. God kept them healthy and strong. Draw vegetables for the boys to eat. How does God help keep you healthy?

What did Zechariah write on the tablet when his baby boy was born?
Unscramble the words and write them on the blanks.

is His
John name

___ ___ ___

___ ___ ___ ___

___ ___ ___ ___ ___ .

17

Baby Jesus' first bed was a manger filled with hay. Follow the code to color the picture. Then cut out the picture and glue it to a plastic lid. Punch a hole at the top, tie a string through it, and hang up your ornament at Christmas time.

w = blue   y = yellow
x = brown   z = pink

What does the shepherd boy see in the sky? Connect the dots to see.
What good news did the shepherd boy hear?

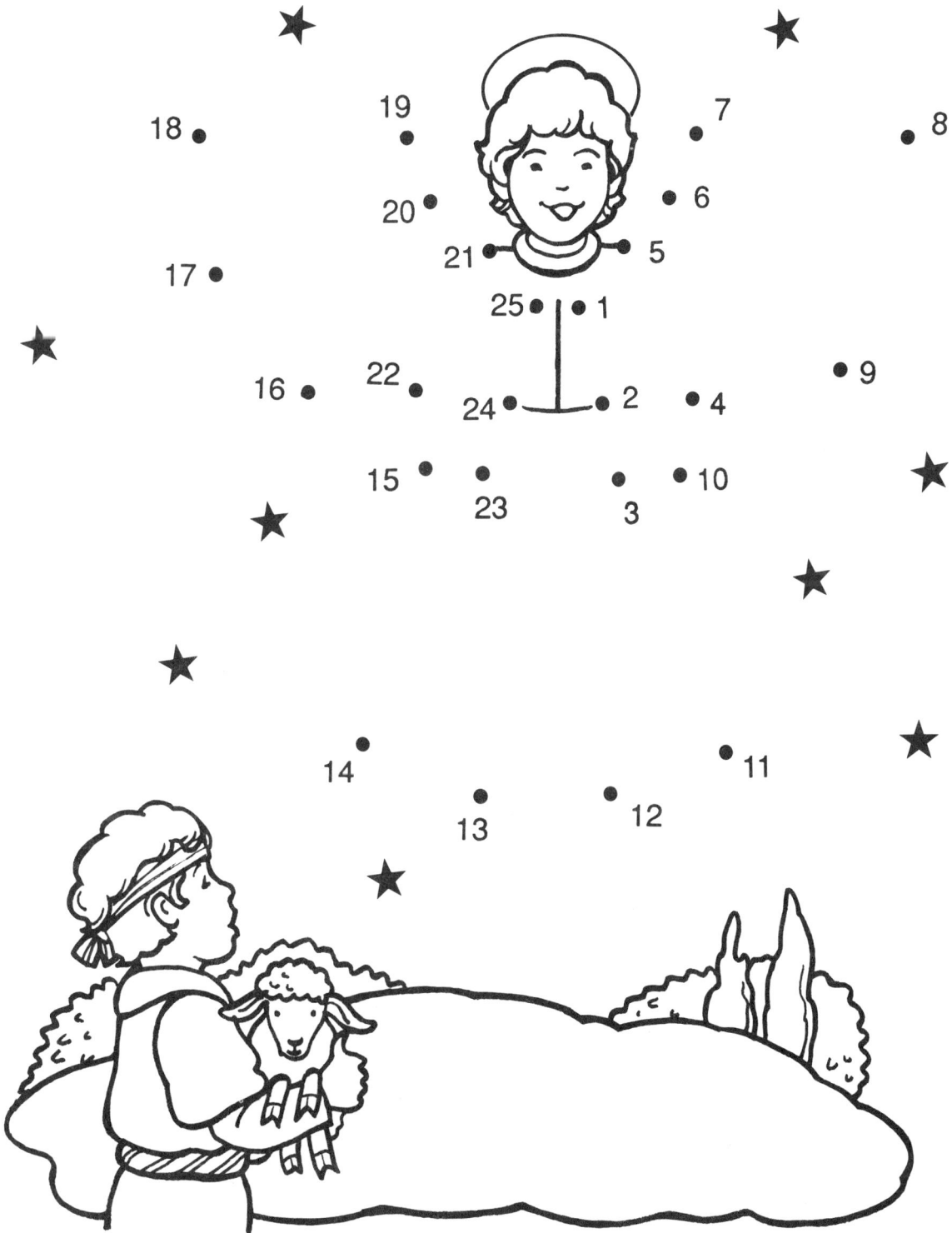

18 •

19 •

7 •

8 •

20 •

6 •

21 •

5 •

17 •

25 • • 1

22 •

16 •

24 • • 2

• 4

• 9

15 •

23 •

10 •

3 •

14 •

11 •

13 •

12 •

19

As Jesus grew up He helped Joseph make things out of wood. Help Jesus pick up the tools He needs. Circle the carpenter's tools hidden in the picture. How do you help your parents at home?

 mallet
 saw
 ax
 hammer
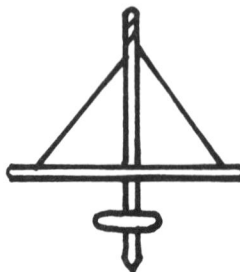 drill
 awl

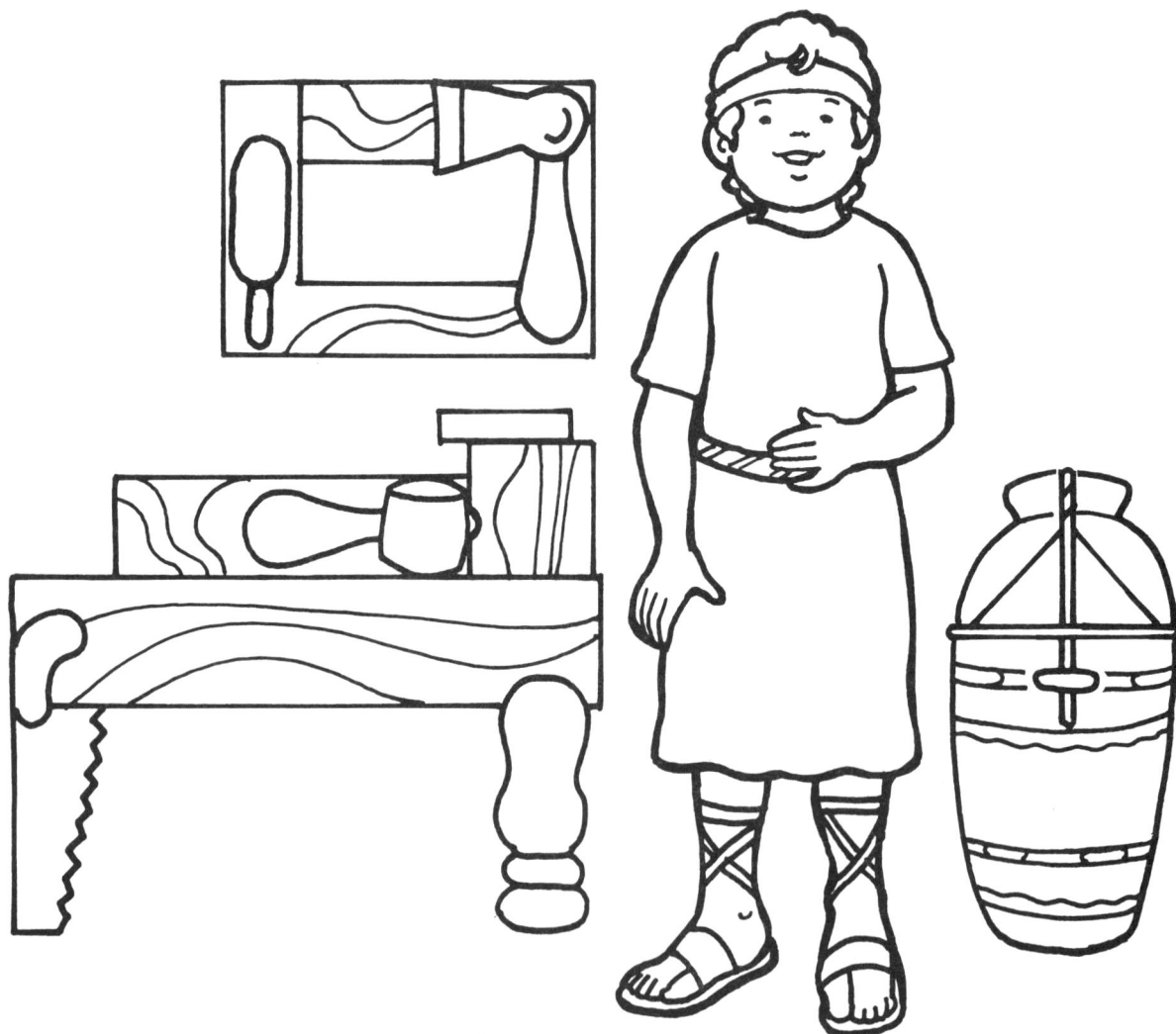

20

When Jesus was 12 years old, Mary and Joseph took Him to the beautiful temple in Jerusalem. Mary and Joseph started home. Then they noticed Jesus was missing. Draw a line to help Mary and Joseph find Jesus. Whose work did Jesus need to do?

The disciples tried to send little children home. But Jesus said, "Let the little children come to Me" (Matthew 19:14). Draw a picture of yourself by Jesus. Thank Him for keeping you close.

22

Jairus asked Jesus to come see his little girl who was very sick. The little girl died. Jesus took the little girl's hand and told her to get up. She was alive again! Draw a picture of the little girl by Jesus and her parents.

23

God helps you to get better when you are sick. Write a story about a time when God helped you get well. Draw a picture to go with it.

Jesus fed over 5,000 people with a little boy's lunch of five loaves of bread and two fish. Color the basket with the right number of loaves and fish. Draw a picture of Jesus beside it.

Children waved palm branches and sang "Hosanna" to Jesus as He rode a donkey into Jerusalem. Connect the dots to see the palm branch the girl is waving.

What did the children sing to Jesus in the temple? Trace the lines that lead from each letter to a circle. Write the correct letter in each circle and read down to find what the children sang. What songs do you like to sing to Jesus?

N
O
H
A
A
N
S

On Good Friday Jesus died on the cross to take the punishment for our sins. His friends were very sad. Draw sad faces for the children. On Easter, Jesus came alive again! His friends were very happy. Draw happy faces for the children. Jesus gives you a new life here on earth, and one day you will live with Him in heaven forever!

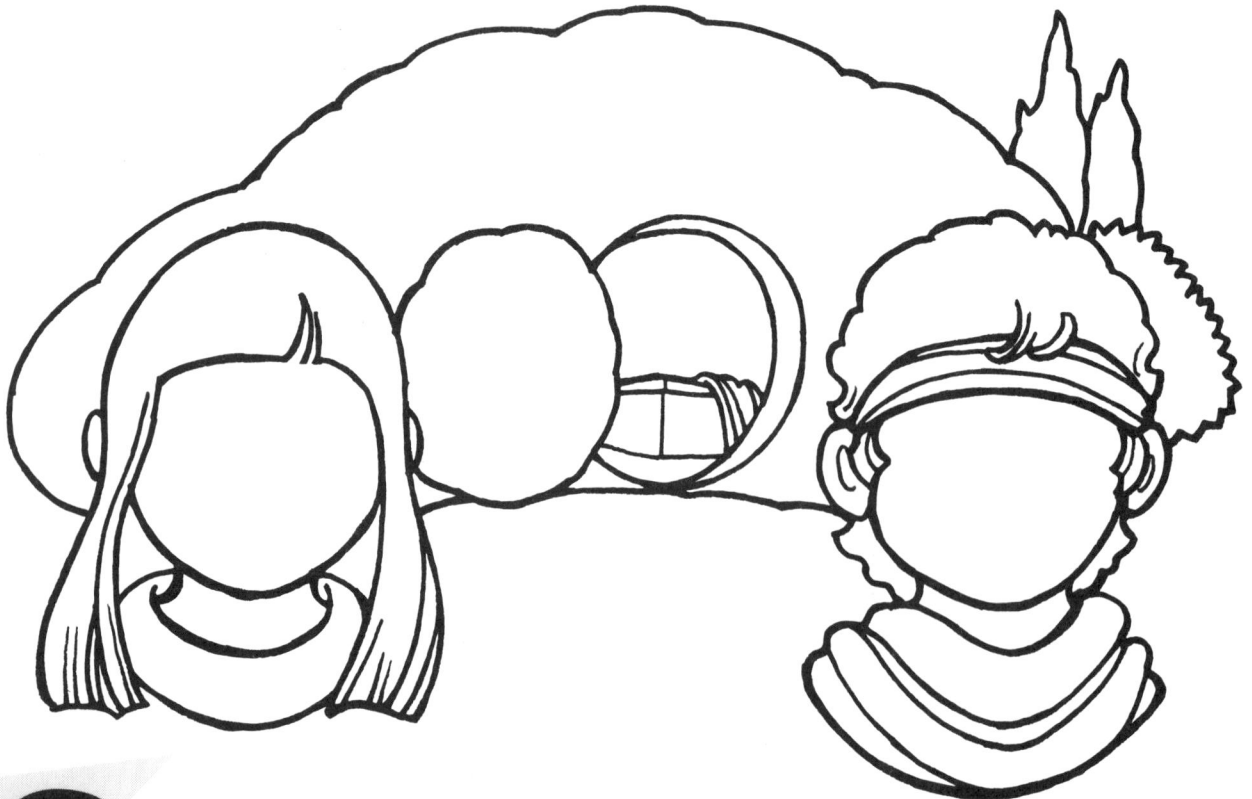

28

Timothy liked to hear grandmother Lois tell him stories from the Bible. What Bible story do you think he is listening to now? Draw a picture of the story, or write it down, in the speech balloon.

29

Copy this page and page 31. Color the cards and cut them out. Deal the cards to yourself and one other player. Place any pairs face-up in front of you. Hold the rest of your cards in your hand. Take turns drawing cards from each other. Whoever has the card of "Jesus and the Children" at the end of the game is the winner.

Jesus and
the Children

Joseph

Moses

Samuel

Miriam

David

30

CPH © 1993

Naaman's Wife

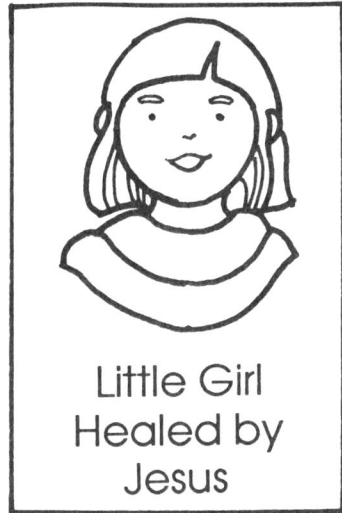

Little Girl Healed by Jesus

Joseph

Moses

Samuel

Miriam

David

Naaman's Wife

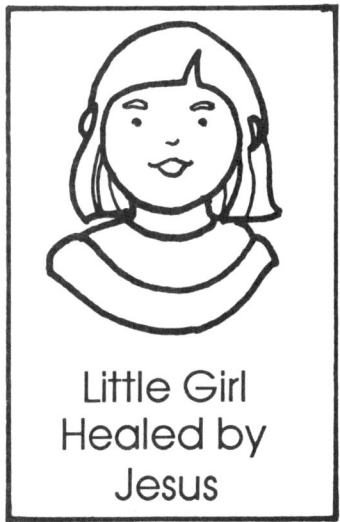

Little Girl Healed by Jesus

31

Dorcas made new clothes for these children. Trace the dots to see the clothes. Decorate them with pretty colors. Can you share God's love by helping someone who needs new clothes or food or toys?